The Magic School Bus
in the Time
of the Dinosaurs

The Magic School Bus
in the Time of the Dinosaurs

By Joanna Cole
Illustrated by Bruce Degen

The author and illustrator wish to thank
Mark A. Norell, Associate Curator of Vertebrate Paleontology,
the American Museum of Natural History, for his assistance in preparing this book.

For their helpful advice and consultation, thanks also to Armand Morgan,
Public Education Department, Yale-Peabody Museum of Natural History, New Haven, Connecticut;
Professor Leo J. Hickey, Curator of Paleobotany, Yale-Peabody Museum of Natural History;
Dave Varricchio, expert of Tyrannosaurus Rex, Museum of the Rockies, Bozeman, Montana.

Scholastic Children's Books,
7-9 Pratt Street, London NW1 OAE UK
A division of Scholastic Publications Ltd
London ~ New York ~ Toronto ~ Sydney ~ Auckland

First published by Scholastic Inc. 1994
This edition published by Scholastic Ltd. 1995

ISBN: 0 590 54254 0

Typeset by Rapid Reprographics
Printed by Paramount Printing Co, Hong Kong

10 9 8 7 6 5 4 3 2 1

To Armand Morgan,
our personal guide to the time of the dinosaurs
J.C. & B.D.

It was Visitors Day at our school.
Parents, relatives, and friends
were coming that afternoon to see our work.
In Miss Frizzle's class, we were making
the whole room into Dinosaur Land!

DINOSAURS WERE REPTILES
by Carlos

Dinosaurs were a group of special prehistoric reptiles. Reptiles are animals that:
- have backbones
- have scaly skin
- lay eggs
- are cold-blooded

REPTILES OF TODAY

SNAKES

CROCODILES

TURTLES

RELATED TO A DINOSAUR AND PROUD OF IT!

LIZARDS

DINOSAURS WERE SPECIAL

Dinosaurs had straight legs. They could walk or run fast.

Today's reptiles have sprawled-out legs.

"Our class has been invited to a dinosaur dig," explained the Friz.
"We'll be leaving straight away."
As we went out, one kid grabbed the video camera.
Others took along model dinosaurs for good luck.
When you have the wackiest teacher in school,
you need all the luck you can get!

WE'RE LEAVING NOW?

I SUPPOSE MISS FRIZZLE HAS FORGOTTEN ABOUT VISITORS DAY.

SHE'S NEVER FORGOTTEN ANYTHING BEFORE.

Dear Come and see the dinosaur bones we're digging up. Bring the whole class. Yours, Jeff

Miss V. Frizzle SCHOOL U.S.A.

We couldn't believe we had to get on that rickety old school bus again. Kids held their lucky dinosaurs tight, and hoped for the best.

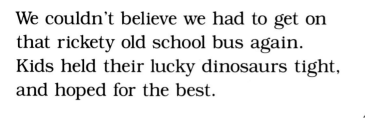

MY LUCKY DINOSAUR IS TYRANNOSAURUS REX.

MY LUCKY DINOSAUR IS STEGOSAURUS.

MY LUCKY DINOSAUR IS WONDERING IF THIS OLD BUS WILL MAKE IT!

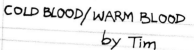

COLD BLOOD/WARM BLOOD
by Tim

COLD-BLOODED animals get most of their body heat from outside their bodies.

We're getting our heat from the sun.

we move slowly in cold weather.

WARM-BLOODED animals make their own body heat.

We are making heat inside our own bodies.

We can move fast even when it's cold.

DINOSAURS WERE SPECIAL
Some dinosaurs may have been warm-blooded. All of today's reptiles are cold-blooded.

NO HUMAN HAS EVER SEEN A DINOSAUR
by Florrie

When early humans appeared on earth, dinosaurs had already been dead for millions of years! People found out about dinosaurs from fossils.

FIVE KINDS OF DINOSAUR FOSSILS
by Alex

1. BONES
2. TEETH
3. FOOTPRINTS
4. SKIN PRINTS
5. EGGS AND NESTS

As we rolled on to the motor way,
Miss Frizzle shouted from the driver's seat,
"We're on our way to fossil country, kids!
Who knows what a fossil is?"
Luckily, we had done our homework.
We knew a fossil is anything left
from a prehistoric animal or plant.

THIS STORY IS MAKE-BELIEVE.

THERE WERE NO DINOSAURS IN THE TIME OF CAVE PEOPLE.

B.C. BOY COMICS
DOG!

After we had been driving for a long time,
we came to a desert where people were working.
Miss Frizzle said this was the dinosaur dig.
The people were paleontologists —
scientists who study prehistoric life.

HOW A DEAD DINOSAUR
COULD BECOME A FOSSIL
by Carmen

1. The dead body sank in a river, and rotted away.

2. The bones were covered with sand.

3. In time, the sand turned into rocks.

4. The bones became hard as rock, too.

DINOSAURS LASTED FOR 150 MILLION YEARS ON EARTH! WEREN'T THEY AMAZING, ARNOLD?

IT'S AMAZING THAT I'VE LASTED THIS LONG IN MISS FRIZZLE'S CLASS.

DID MOST DINOSAURS TURN INTO FOSSILS?

NO! DEAD DINOSAURS USUALLY ROTTED OR WERE EATEN.

DINOSAURS WERE SPECIAL
Dinosaurs were on earth **1500** times longer than humans have been so far.

WHERE HAVE DINOSAUR FOSSILS BEEN FOUND?
by Phil
Everywhere on earth -- even within the Arctic Circle and near the South Pole!

LOOKING FOR DINOSAUR FOSSILS? TRY WESTERN NORTH AMERICA! by Keesha
There are so many dinosaur fossils in the West that the area has been called a fossil treasure trove.

° Fossil Sites

North America

Everyone at the dig was working hard, using all kinds of tools to separate the fossils from the rocks around them.

I SEE YOU'RE STILL INTERESTED IN DINOSAURS, JEFF.

VALERIE! I HAVEN'T SEEN YOU SINCE HIGH SCHOOL!

LET'S GET THIS ON VIDEO!

WHISK BROOM

GLUE

PLASTER

BURLAP

BONE IS WRAPPED WITH BURLAP AND PLASTER SO IT WON'T BREAK WHEN IT IS MOVED.

We saw a gleam in Miss Frizzle's eye.
"Want to look for some *Maiasaura* nests, kids?" she shouted.
She rushed us onto the bus and drove off.

We hadn't gone far when Miss Frizzle stopped the bus.
She turned a dial on the dashboard, and the bus began to change.
It looked like a giant alarm clock.
Miss Frizzle said it was a time machine!

The hand on the clock started moving backwards:
One hour back . . . one day back . . . one year back . . .
Outside the windows, the desert was whizzing by.
One thousand years . . . one million years . . .
"We're on our way to the time of the *Maiasaura*.
Hang on, class!" yelled the Friz.

PRECAMBRIAN

PALEOZOIC ERA

MESOZOIC ERA

CENOZOIC ERA

NOW

MILLIONS OF YEARS AGO

4,600   570   505   438   408   310   286   248   225   213   144   65   1

JELLYFISH
PRECAMBRIAN

TRILOBITES
CAMBRIAN

NAUTILOIDS
ORDOVICIAN

GIANT SEA SCORPIONS
FIRST FISH
SILURIAN

FIRST INSECT
FIRST AMPHIBIANS
DEVONIAN

GREAT FORESTS
CARBONIFEROUS

FIRST REPTILES
SAIL-BACK REPTILES
PERMIAN

ERYTHROSUCHUS
TRIASSIC

ICHTHYOSAUR
PLATEOSAURUS
COELOPHYSIS
LATE TRIASSIC

STEGOSAURUS
DIPLODOCUS
JURASSIC

TRICERATOPS
MAIASAURA
TYRANNOSAURUS REX
CRETACEOUS

WOOLLY MAMMOTH
SABER-TOOTHED TIGER
TERTIARY

QUATERNARY

PRESENT TIME

THE AGE OF DINOSAURS

WHOA!

Ring! Ring! The alarm went off.
We heard Miss Frizzle say, "Ooops!
We had a little machine trouble.
We went back too far in time,
but it's nothing to worry about."
Nothing to worry about!
We missed the time of the *Maiasaura*
by millions of years!

WHAT WAS THE EARTH LIKE THEN?

PANGAEA

One giant continent called PANGAEA

• Rainy Jungles
• Many deserts
• Warm temperatures
• No winter anywhere!

CLASS, WE'RE IN THE LATE TRIASSIC PERIOD-- THE TIME OF THE EARLY DINOSAURS!

YOU MEAN WE'RE IN THE SAME PLACE BUT IN ANOTHER TIME?

YOU MEAN THIS IS WHAT THAT DESERT LOOKED LIKE 220 MILLION YEARS AGO?

WOW! IT'S A JUNGLE OUT THERE!

DINODONTOSAURUS

COELOPHYSIS

WHERE WE ARE IN TIME

PRESENT TIME

CENOZOIC ERA
65 MILLION YEARS AGO

CRETACEOUS
144 MILLION YEARS AGO

JURASSIC
213 MILLION YEARS AGO

LATE TRIASSIC
225 MILLION YEARS AGO

Suddenly, a large reptile rose out of the water and opened its huge mouth.

"That is not a dinosaur," Miss Frizzle said.

"It's a phytosaur — a crocodile-like reptile."

The phytosaur caught a little dinosaur and pulled it underwater.

We wanted to get back on the bus, pronto! But Miss Frizzle said we had to learn about Triassic plant life.

AETOSAUR

PHYTOSAUR

ARE MEAT-EATERS MEAN?
by Arnold
No. Predators are part of nature. Hunting is the only way they can get their food.

SOME WORDS FROM DOROTHY ANN
A predator is a hunting animal.
Prey are the animals a predator hunts.

I'M A PREDATOR.

I'M PREY.

CONIFER

PLATEOSAUR

A sudden downpour caught us by surprise.
But the dinosaurs just went on eating.
We ran for the bus, and Frizzie called,
"Get ready to go *forward* in time, kids!"

IN A TROPICAL FOREST, RAINS ARE FREQUENT AND HEAVY, ARNOLD.

NOW SHE TELLS ME!

JEFF WILL LOVE THIS VIDEO.

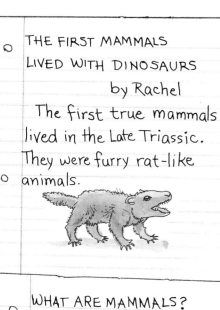

THE FIRST MAMMALS
LIVED WITH DINOSAURS
by Rachel

The first true mammals
lived in the Late Triassic.
They were furry rat-like
animals.

WHAT ARE MAMMALS?
by Wanda

Mammals are animals that:
- have backbones
- have hair or fur
- are warm-blooded

- feed their babies with
mothers' milk

The last things we saw before we took off
were some small, furry animals.
Miss Frizzle said they were the first mammals.
The hand on the clock moved ahead,
and the Triassic rain forest whizzed out of sight.

WHEN WILL WE SEE MAIASAURA EGGS?

MAIASAURA LIVED 160 MILLION YEARS FROM NOW. LET'S SEE IF WE CAN FIND THEM.

EARLY MAMMALS

Ring! Ring! The alarm went off,
and we heard Miss Frizzle say, "Oh no!"
We had stopped too soon.
It was the Late Jurassic Period,
the Age of Giants!

APATOSAURUS
(ALSO CALLED
BRONTOSAURUS)

WHAT WAS THE EARTH LIKE
THEN?

Continents were drifting
apart.
• Swampy, low-lying plains
• Beginnings of inland seas
• Beginning of Atlantic Ocean
• Warm temperatures everywhere

HERE ARE SOME
INTERESTING
TREE TRUNKS.

UM... I DON'T
THINK SO.

WHERE WE ARE IN TIME

PRESENT TIME

CENOZOIC ERA
65 MILLION YEARS AGO

CRETACEOUS
144 MILLION YEARS AGO

JURASSIC
213 MILLION YEARS AGO

LATE TRIASSIC
225 MILLION YEARS AGO

WE KNOW DINOSAURS LAID EGGS
by Amanda Jane
Fossil dinosaur eggs have been found. Inside some, there are tiny skeletons of babies.

HOW BIG WERE DINOSAUR EGGS?
by Molly
The largest dinosaur egg we have found was about the size of a football!

Under a pile of leaves, we found some dinosaur eggs just about to hatch!
Nearby some stegosaurs — plated dinosaurs — were eating plants.
One of the stegosaurs had a hurt leg.

Suddenly an *Allosaurus* approached
the wounded *Stegosaurus*.
Stegosaurus's spiked tail lashed out.
It missed *Allosaurus* by an inch!
What would happen next?
We held our breath.

serrated edge

ALLOSAURUS
TOOTH
(actual size)

IT'S HARD TO BE A HUNTER
by Alex
Being a predator is
dangerous. Predators
can get hurt or killed
by their prey. This is why
meat-eaters often attack
prey that is weak, sick,
or young.

Allosaurus darted close and took a big bite.
Then it moved back and waited.
Stegosaurus got weaker and weaker.
It had become food for Allosaurus.

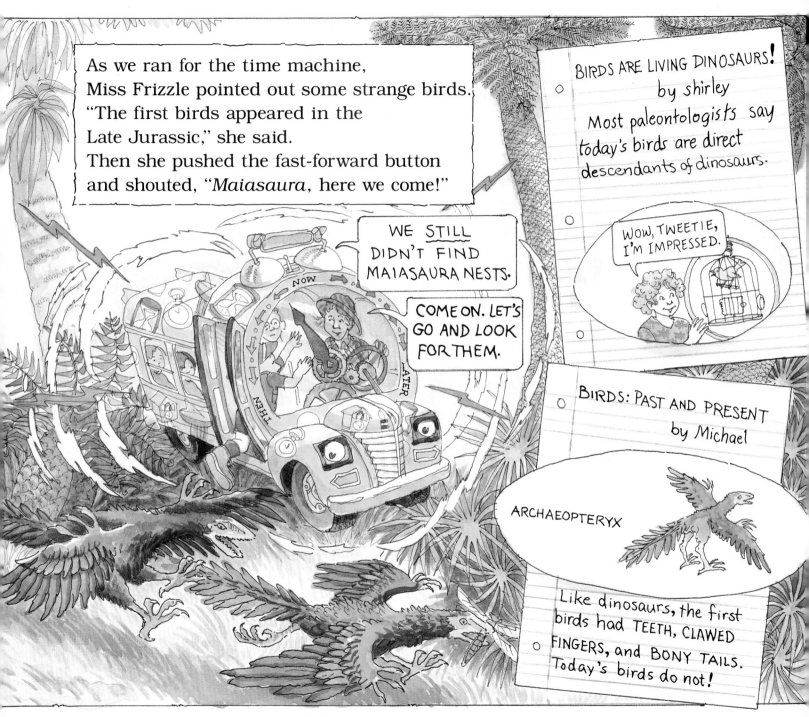

ALL DINOSAURS WERE
__LAND ANIMALS__
          by Gregory
No dinosaurs lived in
the sea. During the
Cretaceous, dinosaurs lived
in places that were not
covered by water.

WE WON'T SEE
ANY DINOSAURS
HERE.

Ring! Ring! The alarm went off again.
We looked out — and then we freaked out!
Once again, we had stopped too soon.
"Here we are in the Late Cretaceous Period,"
announced Miss Frizzle.
"At this time there was a sea
right in the middle of our continent."

WE'RE IN THE
SAME PLACE
25 MILLION
YEARS LATER.

HOW TIME
FLIES.

THAT'S NOT ALL
THAT FLIES.

PTERANODON

WHERE WE ARE IN TIME

PRESENT TIME

CENOZOIC ERA
65 MILLION YEARS AGO

CRETACEOUS
144 MILLION YEARS AGO

JURASSIC
213 MILLION YEARS AGO

LATE TRIASSIC
225 MILLION YEARS AGO

Through the windows, enormous sea reptiles swam by.
Overhead, flying reptiles glided past,
dipping their beaks in the water to catch fish.
We were getting a little wet,
so the Friz set the clock ahead again.

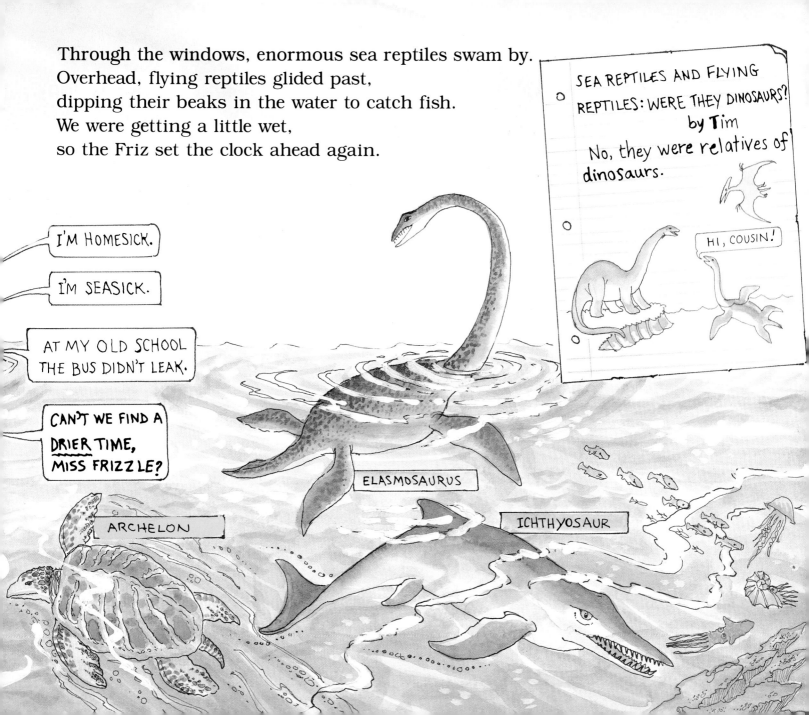

The next thing we knew we had travelled
forward two million years.
Now, we were at the very end
of the Cretaceous Period.
This was the time of the last dinosaurs.
This was the time we had been looking for!

As soon as we got off the bus,
we saw that the Cretaceous world was different.
The weather was cooler.
There were colourful flowers and fruits everywhere.
And there were lots of new plant-eating dinosaurs.
"These plant-eaters could chew better than
any other dinosaurs," said Miss Frizzle.
"They had terrific teeth for grinding,
and they had *cheeks*!"

NEW PLANT-EATERS OF THE CRETACEOUS PERIOD
by Miss Frizzle

DUCKBILLS
Had hundreds of teeth in horny beaks.

DOMEHEADS
Had thick skulls. May have butted heads like rams.

ARMOURED
Had armour Had few teeth.

HORNED
Had neck frill and horns. Had slicing teeth.

CHEEKS KEEP FOOD FROM FALLING OUT SO PLANT-EATERS DO NOT LOSE FOOD THEY HAVE ALREADY CHEWED.

I DIDN'T KNOW CHEEKS WERE SO IMPORTANT.

DINOSAURS WERE SPECIAL
Some dinosaurs chewed their food. All of today's reptiles swallow it whole.

DUCKBILL TEETH
Duckbills had hundreds of rows of teeth.

We were watching the plant-eaters chew, when some tyrannosaurs approached. Tyrannosaurs were the largest meat-eaters ever. Their mouths were giant biting machines with sixty sharp, stabbing teeth!

The tyrannosaurs were scary enough.
Then a pack of *Troodon* showed up, too!
They were small, but there were a lot of them!
They began circling the bus to see what it was.
We sized up the situation and ran.

As we came over the crest of a hill,
we saw an incredible sight!
It was the *Maiasaura* nesting ground!

WHY DO WE THINK MAIASAURA BABIES GREW UP IN NESTS?

by Wanda

When scientists found the first Maiasaura nests, they saw:

- <u>Crushed eggshells</u>, showing that babies might have stayed in nests and stepped on shells.
- <u>Skeletons of different sizes</u>, showing that babies might have grown bigger in nests.

- <u>Worn down baby teeth</u>, showing that babies might have eaten food brought by parents.

We weren't the only ones
who had found the *Maiasaura*.
The *Troodon* had followed us.
They invaded the nesting ground.
The *Maiasaura* parents defended their young.
All at once, a sandstorm blew up.
In minutes, a thick layer of sand
covered the dinosaurs.

Everything happened so fast.
There was no way we could help
the dinosaurs.
Maybe they would become fossils.

OH, NO!
I DROPPED
MY MODEL
MAIASAURA!

HURRY UP
AND RUN!

Back in the bus, Miss Frizzle
drove forward in time.
We thought we were going home,
but, on the way,
the bus screeched to a stop.

STRUTHIOMIMUS

PRESENT TIME

CENOZOIC ERA
65 MILLION YEARS AGO

CRETACEOUS
144 MILLION YEARS AGO

JURASSIC
213 MILLION YEARS AGO

LATE TRIASSIC
225 MILLION YEARS AGO

WHERE WE ARE IN TIME

"We are in the very last minutes of the Cretaceous Period," said Miss Frizzle. A bright light was shining in the sky. "Notice that asteroid," said the Friz. "It's a huge rock from outer space. Soon it will hit the earth."

THE ASTEROID WILL CAUSE AN ENORMOUS EXPLOSION... BLACK SOOT WILL FILL THE AIR AND BLOCK OUT THE SUN... PLANTS WON'T GROW, AND MILLIONS OF LIVING THINGS WILL BECOME EXTINCT — INCLUDING THE DINOSAURS.

MISS FRIZZLE, COULD WE LEAVE BEFORE THE ASTEROID HITS?

LAMBEOSAURUS

The Friz pushed the forward button, and we started again.

WE'RE ONLY 65 MILLION YEARS FROM HOME, CLASS.

STEP ON IT, PLEASE...

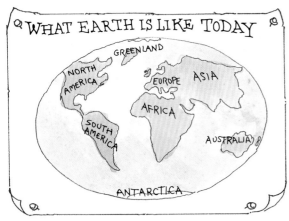

In the classroom, we made a chart
of our trip to the dinosaurs.
Just as we were finishing it,
people started coming in for Visitors Day.

The visitors admired everything.
They had never seen such fabulous projects,
such wonderful books, or such an incredible video.
And, of course, they had never met a teacher
quite like Miss Frizzle!